MAKING DECISIONS

ROBERT HELLER

DK PUBLISHING, INC.

A DK PUBLISHING BOOK

Project Editor Sasha Heseltine
Project Art Editor Darren Hill
Editor Marian Broderick
US Editor Leonard C. Hort
Designer Austin Barlow

DTP Designer Jason Little
Production Controllers Silvia La Greca,
Michelle Thomas

Series Editor Jane Simmonds
Series Art Editor Tracy Hambleton-Miles

Managing Editor Stephanie Jackson
Managing Art Editor Nigel Duffield

First American Edition, 1998
2 4 6 8 10 9 7 5 3 1

Published in the United States by
DK Publishing, Inc.
95 Madison Avenue
New York, New York 10016

Visit us on the World Wide Web at http://www.dk.com

Library of Congress Cataloging-in-Publication Data

Heller, Robert, 1932–
    Making decisions / by Robert Heller
        p.   cm. -- (Essential managers)
    Includes index.
    ISBN 0-7894-2889-X
    1. Decision-making.   2. Industrial management--
Decision-making.   3. Leadership.
4. Strategic planning   I. Title.   II. Series.
HD30.23.H4465   1998
658.4'03--dc21   98–18011
                                                  CIP

Reproduced by Colourscan, Singapore
Printed and bound in Italy by Graphicom srl

CONTENTS

IMPLEMENTING A DECISION

INTRODUCTION

Decisions are an essential part of life – in and out of a work environment. Decision makers are those who are responsible for making a judgment – sometimes a crucial judgment – between two or more alternatives. Making Decisions *takes you through the whole process of making good, effective decisions, from initial deliberation to final implementation. It is suitable for anyone making work-related choices, whether they are new to decision-making or are seasoned managers. Information is provided on generating ideas, forecasting, assessing risks, and dealing with personnel issues. The book includes a self-assessment exercise, which allows you to judge your own decision-making abilities, and has 101 practical tips containing further vital information.*

ANALYZING DECISION-MAKING

Part of a manager's role is needing to make a series of large and small decisions. Reaching the right decision in every situation is an ambition that is well worth striving to achieve.

DEFINING DECISIONS

A decision is a judgment or choice between two or more alternatives, and arises in an infinite number of situations, from the resolution of a problem to the implementation of a course of action. Managers of people, by definition, must be decision makers.

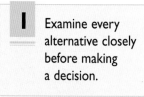

1 Examine every alternative closely before making a decision.

2 If you find that previous decisions are still workable, make use of them.

WHO MAKES DECISIONS?

A decision is a choice between a variety of alternatives, and a decision maker is whoever makes such a choice. A decision can be made instantly but more often involves the decision-maker in a process of identification, analysis, assessment, choice, and planning. To arrive at a decision, a manager must define the purpose of the action, list the options available, choose between the options, and then turn that choice into action. Decisions and the process of decision-making are fundamental to all management processes – just as they are to everyday life.

CATEGORIZING DECISIONS

The various types of decision a manager has to make include routine, emergency, strategic, and operational. Many decisions are routine: the same circumstances recur, and when they arise you choose a proven course of action. Some situations, however, are without precedent – you make the decision on the spot as events unfold. This is emergency decision-making and can take up most of a manager's time. The most demanding form of decision-making involves strategic choices; deciding on aims and objectives, and converting these into specific plans, or subdecisions, is a manager's most important task. Operational decisions, especially those concerned with "people problems" (including hiring and firing), require particularly sensitive handling.

3 Make long-term decisions with the short term in mind.

4 Change decisions that are no longer appropriate.

▼ **REACHING DECISIONS BY CONSENSUS**
Discussing a problem with colleagues is often the best way to move toward a decision. When people get together, they often come up with unexpected solutions.

Colleague's contribution adds to creative process

Manager explains alternative solutions

Colleague pays close attention to proceedings

BREAKING DOWN THE PROCESS

Reaching a decision involves a methodical thought process. The first step is to identify the exact issue that is being tackled, and to prioritize objectives. An analysis of the situation will reveal those options that are impossible or impractical to implement, leaving a manageable range of alternatives for more detailed assessment. At this stage – if not earlier – others' views may be enlisted. The advantages and disadvantages of each course of action should be carefully evaluated, always keeping the ultimate goal in the forefront. Finally, a plan can be devised to show exactly how the decision will be carried out.

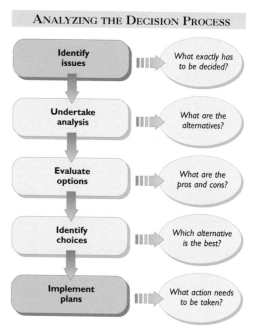

ANALYZING THE DECISION PROCESS

Identify issues → What exactly has to be decided?

Undertake analysis → What are the alternatives?

Evaluate options → What are the pros and cons?

Identify choices → Which alternative is the best?

Implement plans → What action needs to be taken?

5 Consider the implications of each decision – they can be huge.

6 Try to foresee and prepare for any changes in a situation.

COMPARING SOLUTIONS

Most decision-making involves problem-solving, and managers arrive at their answers in a wide variety of ways. For example, there might be a clear and correct answer (based on facts and figures); there might be an insight that feels right (based on experience); there might be a solution that you need to test by carrying it out (or carrying out a simulation of it); there might be a solution that works in the short term but not in the long term (such as throwing money at a scheduling problem); or there might be a fuzzy solution – one that seems to work but does not have clear boundaries (such as launching a new product and waiting to see if it changes the parameters of the marketplace).

UNDERSTANDING RISKS

Most decisions involve an element of risk, though some are less risky than others. Sometimes, even when theoretical options exist, their disadvantages are so great that there is no real alternative. This may arise from a bad original decision. For example, an organization has overstretched itself financially by deciding to invest in a new factory. It could decide to halt the project, but only at the risk of immediate financial collapse. That may be averted if the new plant eventually meets its targets. Therefore, to retreat is riskier than to proceed. Also, remember to watch for side effects. Cutting staff may seem a safe decision, but not if it risks deterioration in customer service.

7 Always ask what can go wrong when you are making a decision.

EVALUATING SOLUTIONS

Sometimes the risks involved in a decision can be reduced by testing, either in the marketplace or by simulation. For example, if a new product on the market has a problem – such as if it has missed its target and is losing money, – you can look at some possible solutions and simulate the financial outcome of each:

● Closing production down at once to prevent further financial loss;
● Carrying on marketing the product with renewed vigor but along the same lines;
● Replacing the management team and having the new team review the marketing campaigns;
● Redesigning the product and starting the campaign again from scratch;
● Selling the product to another company and developing a new product.

The correct decision in any case must be the one that offers the best prospects for the long-term future, because long-term success is naturally the ultimate aim of any manager.

QUESTIONS TO ASK YOURSELF

Q What are our short- and long-term objectives?

Q Will we make money with this product/service/idea?

Q How much energy do we need to put into marketing?

Q Do we need to recruit new people?

Q What happens if the marketplace changes?

Q What are our worst-case scenarios, and how would we deal with them?

8 Always consider all the possible outcomes when making a decision.

IDENTIFYING DECISION-MAKING STYLES

People have individual styles of making decisions. Whether your style is logical or creative, your method should also be rational and straightforward. Good decision makers do not allow personality to control the decision process or its outcome.

9 Always try to balance an intuitive hunch with sound logical analysis.

10 Assess your decision-making abilities, and strive to improve them.

USING HUNCH AND LOGIC

One side of the brain is believed to be the location of emotion, imagination, intuition, and creativity; the other is the site of logic, language, math, and analysis. Though people tend to have a dominant side, this does not mean that decision makers fall into two separate categories: the intuitive decision maker deciding creatively and spontaneously, versus the logical decision maker working rationally on fact-based judgment. Whichever side your natural decision-making style leans toward, always aim to achieve a balance between both sets of faculties.

ASSESSING THE ▼ THINKING PROCESS
Whether the intuitive or rational side of your brain dominates your thinking processes, both can contribute to forming a balanced picture.

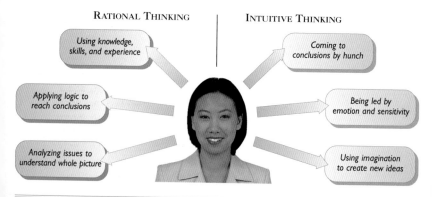

RATIONAL THINKING | INTUITIVE THINKING

Using knowledge, skills, and experience

Applying logic to reach conclusions

Analyzing issues to understand whole picture

Coming to conclusions by hunch

Being led by emotion and sensitivity

Using imagination to create new ideas

TAKING RISKS

Risk-taking is not just for the intuitive – any decision with an uncertain outcome involves some element of risk, and even people who are totally logical in their thinking take risks. Much of the difference between the two methods of reaching a decision lies in the mental approach: intuitive thinkers back an option that they are convinced is a certainty, although it may seem to others to be a long shot, while logical thinkers calculate all the odds and only then make their decision to go for the best option. Either way, seek to minimize the degree of risk involved.

BEING SYSTEMATIC

Whatever your decision-making style, there are advantages in being systematic. Systematic methods of reaching a decision ensure that all the correct issues are addressed: necessary information is gathered, all alternatives are properly considered and compared, difficulties are identified and feasibility assessed, and consequences are taken fully into account. A systematic approach enables you to prepare a logical and effective plan of action so that your decision process can be explained clearly to any colleagues or clients who are affected.

11 Avoid making decisions that have a large element of chance in them.

REVIEWING PRECEDENTS

People often repeat what has previously worked well. This can lead to very good performance, since repetition improves effectiveness. At some point, however, needs may change, and a previously correct decision becomes wrong or less appropriate. The antidote is to approach your decision like a first-time choice. What would a newcomer decide? If, after putting yourself in this position, it feels wrong to follow precedent, it is probably time to innovate.

12 Follow a precedent when it works – but not when it doesn't.

KNOWING YOUR CORPORATE CULTURE

A powerful ingredient in decision-making is the corporate culture of your organization. This affects the issues and options available to you when making a decision. Learn what is acceptable to your organization and what is always ruled out.

13 Challenge the company culture in the cause of good decision-making.

14 Make sure that you are known for coming up with good, creative, innovative ideas.

ANALYZING DIFFERENT CORPORATE STYLES

Decisions are affected by, and impact on, the surrounding organization. If your corporate culture is authoritarian and conformist, you are probably bound by bureaucracy, and your ability to make dynamic decisions will be restricted. In contrast, an innovative and progressive company will expect you to be more adventurous, making decisions on your own initiative. With companies that alternate between being risk-averse and ambitious, try to sense the prevailing climate and act accordingly.

OVERCOMING RESISTANCE

The artful decision maker learns to manipulate the system when necessary. For example, the risk-taking organization's bold decisions may have to be curbed if they outrun the available resources, and the risk-averse company may sometimes need to be coaxed into taking unprecedented action in order to stay ahead of the competition. In either case, try to identify the levers of power and influence and form firm alliances with those individuals who are best placed to overcome the various obstacles you may encounter.

15 Marry intellect with intuition in decision-making.

16 Be aware of the politics behind decision-making.

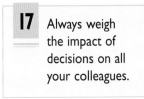

17 Always weigh the impact of decisions on all your colleagues.

◀ **ENCOURAGING CREATIVITY**

Creativity flourishes and individuals use their initiative confidently in an atmosphere of equality, where team spirit exists between staff at all levels.

WHAT CULTURE DOMINATES YOUR ORGANIZATION?

To assess whether your organization tends to be risk-averse or adventurous or is a mixture of the two – overcautious some of the time and overconfident the rest – read through the statements in the columns below and see which of them best fit the company culture.

RISK-AVERSE:
- New ideas are often dismissed.
- The organization is not always driven by external needs.
- The emphasis within the organization is on dealing with problems.
- Stability and experience are the most valued attributes of the organization.
- The good of the company is put before the success of the individual.
- Command and control appear to be the dominant processes.
- It is almost impossible to change the corporate mind-set.

If you agree with most of the definitions above, your company is definitely averse to taking risks. Decisions involving new ideas and technologies are not welcomed readily.

ADVENTUROUS:
- New and creative ideas are welcomed.
- The organization focuses mainly on the needs of the customer.
- The corporate emphasis is on taking advantage of new opportunities.
- Motivation and innovation are among the most valued characteristics.
- Corporate and individual aims are largely aligned.
- All staff are allowed autonomy and are able to show their initiative.
- Minds and policies are frequently changed, according to circumstances.

If you agree with most of the definitions above, your company is forward-thinking, not afraid of change, and happy to accept bold decisions that create success.

ANALYZING YOUR RESPONSIBILITY

Top-down decision-making leads to the delegation of work to subordinate levels. This is natural in hierarchies, but you must decide which decisions to make yourself and which to delegate to others. The best decision makers share responsibility widely.

18 Avoid clinging possessively to a decision that you have delegated.

19 Always give your reasons if rejecting a decision made by a delegate.

MAKING YOUR OWN DECISIONS

It is up to you to decide which decisions are yours alone. Assess what decisions your subordinates are capable of making. If the answer is none, either your assessment of the situation or your initial recruitment must be at fault. Assess which aspects of your role have the greatest impact on outcomes. Retain decisions concerned with these aspects yourself and delegate the rest. Retaining a decision does not mean monopolizing the process – allow your delegates to participate in the decision-making while accepting that you have the final choice.

DELEGATING DECISIONS

Remember that you remain responsible for the decisions you delegate, so oversee the delegation, particularly in sensitive areas. Use that overview for coaching and monitoring; try to build up the confidence of the people you delegate to, maintain a two-way flow of information, and encourage people to develop their own initiative. Do not second-guess or countermand unless absolutely necessary. If you are occasionally forced to reject a decision, explain why in detail.

20 Build up your trust in the ability of other people to make decisions.

PUSHING DECISIONS DOWN

When analyzing responsibilities, it is clear that those closest to the point of action should also make the decisions. For example, mortgage applications are best approved at branch level, plant modifications are best decided on the factory floor, recruitment is best done by those with whom the recruit will work, and so on. Information at the sharp end is likely to be specific and up-to-date. Those who have to live with decisions should participate in them. Sending decisions upward causes delays – the more hierarchical layers there are, the greater the delays. Pushing decisions down pays off in speed and efficiency. Though delegates need to be monitored, they will soon grow into their roles.

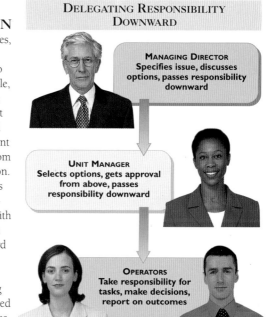

DELEGATING RESPONSIBILITY DOWNWARD

MANAGING DIRECTOR
Specifies issue, discusses options, passes responsibility downward

UNIT MANAGER
Selects options, gets approval from above, passes responsibility downward

OPERATORS
Take responsibility for tasks, make decisions, report on outcomes

◄ LETTING PEOPLE MAKE DECISIONS

In this example, people were delegated to make decisions, initiated action, and implemented their decisions. Things became unworkable in the face of unhelpful interference from others. Given permission to handle their own decisions once again, the team moved ahead successfully.

CASE STUDY

John, an engineering boss, sent a shop-floor team to one of his competitors to see what improvements could be made to part of his operation. The team came back enthusiastic about several innovations and was told to go ahead with decisions on changes required to improve productivity and then to implement them.

Performance began to deteriorate immediately, and a subsequent investigation revealed that managers and senior engineers, hearing about the changes, had descended on the unit, second-guessing decisions that had been made by the shop-floor team.

John was incensed and ordered everybody to stay away from the operation. The shop-floor team was allowed to implement its original decisions, the decline in production was reversed, and the promised gains in productivity were achieved.

BEING DECISIVE

The ability to make timely, clear, and firm decisions is an essential quality of leadership. But the type of decision needed will vary according to the circumstances. As a manager, you need to recognize the implications of making different decisions.

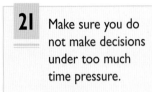

21 Make sure you do not make decisions under too much time pressure.

BEING POSITIVE

Taking decisive action does not mean making decisions on the spur of the moment. Although that may sometimes be necessary in emergencies, and occasionally desirable for other reasons – for example, if the right decision is obvious – the correct definition of "decisive" in this context is "positive." The true leader must approach decisions confidently, being aware of what must be taken into account and fully in command of the decision-making process. Understand what kind of decision is required from you, and do not be afraid to change the decision if circumstances subsequently alter.

Concentrate on assessing your options

▲ **TAKING YOUR TIME**
Do not make a decision immediately unless the solution is obvious. Study all the options open to you and weigh up all the pros and cons.

22 If and when decisions misfire, take fast action.

23 Never postpone vital decisions – make them quickly.

MAKING FAST DECISIONS

It often seems that the most important aspect of a decision is whether it can be made quickly or whether it can wait. For example, if a customer demands an instant discount, you have to decide on the spot whether it is worth conceding for future goodwill. On the other hand, if you are considering a program of price cuts, you can offer discounts to valued customers in a more considered way. Good decision makers often make instant decisions – but they then assess the long-term implications.

TYPES OF DECISION-MAKING

CHARACTERISTICS	IMPLICATIONS
IRREVERSIBLE The decision, once made, cannot be unmade – such as when signing an agreement to sell or buy a company.	● Commits you irrevocably when there is no other satisfactory option to the chosen course. ● Should never be used as an all-or-nothing instant escape from general indecision.
REVERSIBLE The decision can be changed completely – either before, during, or after the agreed action begins.	● Allows you to acknowledge a mistake early in the process rather than perpetuate it. ● Can be used when you see that circumstances may change, so that reversal may be necessary.
EXPERIMENTAL The decision is not final until the first results appear and prove themselves to be satisfactory.	● Requires positive feedback before you can decide on a course of action. ● Useful and effective when correct move is unclear but general direction of action is understood.
TRIAL-AND-ERROR Taken in knowledge that changes in plans will be forced by what actually happens in the course of action.	● Allows you to adapt and adjust plans continually before full and final commitment. ● Uses positive and negative feedback before you continue with a particular course of action.
MADE IN STAGES After the initial step, further decisions follow as each stage of agreed action is completed.	● Allows close monitoring of risks, as you accumulate evidence of outcomes and obstacles at every stage. ● Permits feedback and further discussion before the next stage of the decision is made.
CAUTIOUS Decision allows for contingencies and problems that may crop up later. Decision makers hedge their bets.	● Limits the risks inherent in decision-making, but also may limit the final gains. ● Allows you to scale down projects that look too risky in the first instance.
CONDITIONAL Decision altered if certain foreseen circumstances arise. An "either/or" decision, with options kept open.	● Prepares you to react if the competition makes a new move or if the game plan changes radically. ● Enables you to react quickly to the ever-changing circumstances of today's competitive markets.
DELAYED Put on hold until decision makers feel the time is right. Go-ahead given when required elements are in place.	● Prevents you from making a decision at the wrong time or before all the facts are known. ● May mean that you miss opportunities in the market that needed fast action.

REACHING A DECISION

Mastering the processes and methods involved in making decisions goes a long way toward maximizing your effectiveness and efficiency as a manager.

IDENTIFYING ISSUES

It is crucial to diagnose problems correctly. Before any decision can be made, identify and define the issue and its boundaries clearly. This also means identifying who else needs to be involved in the issue, and analyzing what their involvement means.

24 Approach different types of decision in different ways for good results.

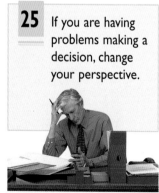

25 If you are having problems making a decision, change your perspective.

UNDERSTANDING WHY A DECISION NEEDS MAKING

Most managerial decisions are prompted by one of four different types of event, each requiring a particular decision-making style:

● Disturbances – manager decides on the best way to solve problems, emergencies, and upheavals;
● Opportunities – manager decides which new openings to pursue and how;
● Resource allocation – manager arbitrates in the distribution of money, personnel, or supplies;
● Negotiations – manager makes decisions as a representative of an organization or individuals.

QUESTIONS TO ASK YOURSELF

Q Have I looked at all the issues involved in the scenario?

Q Have I looked at problematical issues objectively?

Q Are my decisions approached rationally or emotionally?

Q Are my decisions suited to each individual issue?

Q Have I identified issues that tend to recur?

TACKLING WHOLE ISSUES

Decisions that tackle only one specific part of a problem tend to fail. Any decision affects a component or components in an entire business system. Consider whether the issue in question is company-wide or an isolated incident. For example, you can remove one difficult employee, but if the problem is caused by bad management or a bad recruitment policy, nothing has been truly resolved. Do some research; dig deep to find out why a decision is required. This establishes the correct boundaries – and leads to superior results.

CONSULTING OTHERS

In addition to identifying issues, as a decision maker you need to identify the individuals involved. List everybody who would be significantly affected by a decision, such as those in higher management with decision powers of their own; other departments whose work would be affected; and clients and suppliers. Assess who you need to consult to ensure support and goodwill. When you reach a decision, make sure that everybody on your list knows what you have decided and why, whether you have consulted them or not.

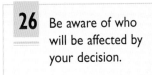

26 Be aware of who will be affected by your decision.

▼ INFORMING COLLEAGUES
Any workplace decision will affect other people in other parts of the organization. Ensure that departments are working together by keeping colleagues informed of proceedings.

IDENTIFYING A TIMESCALE

When you are making a decision, be aware of the timescale involved, but remember that the quality of thinking and execution, rather than the time available, must be the key factor. You should reach your decision without undue haste but also without unnecessary delays. The right time to make your decision is when all the information is in and all the issues have been addressed. Delay is beneficial only if you need to obtain more vital information or if circumstances change and issues have to be reassessed. Time pressure can, in fact, be helpful – it concentrates the mind, rules out procrastination, and reduces the number of alternatives that can be considered.

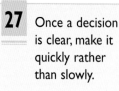

27 Once a decision is clear, make it quickly rather than slowly.

28 Avoid rushing an important decision just because others expect it.

▼ PARETO ANALYSIS

Applied to problem analysis, Pareto's law suggests 80 percent of a problem results from 20 percent of the factors involved (A), so 80 percent of the factors involved account for 20 percent of the problem (B).

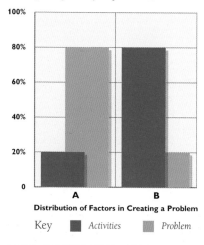

Distribution of Factors in Creating a Problem

Key ■ *Activities* ■ *Problem*

PRIORITIZING FACTORS

When making a decision, prioritize significant factors. Common sense suggests that some factors in a process are more important than others – and analysis supports this. In reality, only 20 percent of activities may account for up to 80 percent of results. This is known as Pareto's law, the "80/20 rule," or the principle of the "vital few and the trivial many." When decision-making, use Pareto's law to sort your priorities. Giving every factor affecting a decision equal weight makes sense only if every factor is equally important; Pareto's law concentrates on the significant 20 percent and gives the less important 80 percent lower priority. When decision-making, divide relevant factors into categories. Prioritize them correctly, and allocate time and effort accordingly so that vital aspects of a decision are not rushed and immaterial aspects do not consume too much time.

THINKING STRATEGICALLY

Before you make a strategic decision, you must first gain a full understanding of the current situation. Get to know the general environment, comparative performances, external requirements, root causes of any performance gaps, and the price of inaction. This five-stage "business case" works for both giants and small units. In any organization, there are questions you can ask yourself, such as:

- What is happening in the marketplace, and how does it work against us?
- Where and why are we underperforming when compared with our competition?
- What do our customers demand that we are unable to supply?
- What causes shortfalls in our performance?
- What negative results will follow if we do not take action immediately?

29 Be optimistic – but remain realistic – when planning your future objectives.

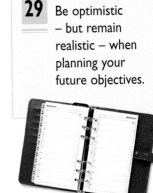

30 Be honest and objective when describing the current situation.

▼ IDENTIFYING PROBLEMS

The first half of making a strategic plan is seeking the positive side of a negative situation. Only after you have identified and analyzed any shortfalls can you make the decisions that will take the organization to where you want it to be.

DECIDING WHERE TO GO

In an ideal situation, you work out where you want your organization to be, and then you make the necessary decisions to get there. Do this firstly by identifying shortfalls and setting them in context, and secondly by setting out the actions necessary to close the gaps. These actions will include:

- Correcting underperformance;
- Meeting customers' requirements;
- Removing the causes of shortcomings;
- Replacing threatened negative results with large benefits.

Each of these actions requires further decisions, all of which are made within the overall decision to get from A (unacceptable) to B (excellence).

| Identify the problem | ➔ | Find out where you are | ➔ | Decide where you want to be |

DECIDING WHOM TO INVOLVE IN A DECISION

Whom to involve, and how, is your very first decision as a decision maker. The number of people you can involve ranges from none, when you make a decision single-handedly, to all, when you lead a whole team searching for consensus.

31 Involve as many people as you need in making a decision.

POINTS TO REMEMBER

- Superiors and subordinates alike enjoy expressing their views.
- People implement decisions more willingly when they have participated in them.
- Collective decisions need not be slow decisions.
- The role of superiors should be clarified before the decision-making process is started.

USING ADVISERS

The arguments for making collective decisions are powerful. The saying that "Two (or more) heads are better than one" is a good one, although this can be countered by the maxim that "Too many cooks spoil the broth." However, in most cases, advisers supply expertise and experience – so there is a clear need for other "cooks." For example, a computing decision will need an IT expert. Ideally, this specific expertise would be supplemented by the experience of a person who has dealt with similar issues.

However, the decision maker, having weighed the advice of the experts and the experienced hands, must then use authority to ensure that a decision is seen through.

◄ **CHOOSING CAREFULLY**
This method of decision-making was successful because, although the manager made the final decision, she consulted both outside experts and colleagues with relevant experience.

CASE STUDY

A manager wanted to remove a production bottleneck by reorganizing one of her departments. After thinking extensively about whom to involve in the process, she decided to call on outside consultants because of their expertise in the department's processes. She also asked the advice of her colleagues Ali, who had several years' experience of working in the department, and Marty, who had led change teams successfully in the past and had considerable authority. She also involved her own team members in a planning group to win cooperation.

The advice and input of Ali, with his in-depth view of the project, Marty's experience in planning the project, the contribution of the staff, plus the technical expertise of the outside consultants, meant that the reorganization was successfully completed.

VETTING DECISIONS

If you do not have full autonomy to proceed, make sure you consult the relevant authority – not just for the ultimate blessing, but also for input. It is always in your interest to have your plans vetted by any senior colleagues whose judgment and experience you trust. Even if you do not need to have your decision sanctioned by your managers, remember that they are much more likely to lend valuable cooperation if they have been kept fully informed all the way along the decision path.

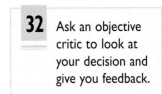

32 Ask an objective critic to look at your decision and give you feedback.

INVOLVING OTHERS IN DECISION-MAKING

METHODS	CHARACTERISTICS	WHEN TO USE THEM
LOW INVOLVEMENT These decisions are made by senior management and are low on consultation.	Telling: manager makes unilateral decision without consultation.	When there is a tight deadline, or in an emergency situation.
	Selling: manager makes decision, but others may question validity.	When a hard sell is needed because consensus is impossible.
	Presenting: staff are allowed to hear the progress of discussions.	When a manager has strong views but wishes to inform colleagues.
MEDIUM INVOLVEMENT Although the final decision is made by the manager, staff are consulted for their input.	Suggesting: manager puts forward choices for discussion and may be willing to change opinion.	When the views of colleagues can contribute useful options for discussion and decision.
	Consulting: colleagues' views are sought before any input from above, but manager has final say.	When a decision needs specialist input or other contributions that a manager needs to have.
HIGH INVOLVEMENT Decision-making is a democratic process, with all staff being invited to participate.	Asking: manager establishes parameters to be discussed, but responsibility rests with team.	When the best decision requires the input and full involvement of the team.
	Participating: all staff come together to discuss options and make decisions by consensus.	When commitment to the decision is of vital importance to the success of the plan.

CONSULTING EFFECTIVELY

Consulting with team members can improve the effectiveness of a decision in two ways: first, the people you approach for their opinions should be able to make a real contribution to the process. Second, the chances of implementing your decision successfully are always increased if people know what they are doing and why; most people operate better if they feel totally involved in a project. Take care to demonstrate that the contributions and opinions you sought have been taken into account in your final decision.

CULTURAL DIFFERENCES

Different consulting traditions exist in different cultures across the world. *Ringi* is the formal mode of consultation in Japan and has deep cultural roots. Despite their innate respect for seniority and authority, the Japanese do argue their cases with their superiors, but once a consensus decision has been reached, conformity and support is total – as is the tendency throughout Southeast Asia. Americans and the British still have a tendency toward "order-and-obey," or top-down management, even within the top echelons, although a more consultative decision-making system has become increasingly popular in the US and the UK. Though consultative at the top, European corporations remain hierarchical further down the organization and in their decision-making processes.

AVOIDING PITFALLS

Consulting others, in some cases, can have more disadvantages than advantages. First, there is the time factor: the more people consulted, however qualified they are to comment, the longer the decision-making process will take, and the greater the number of people approached, the higher your chances of being confused by contradictory opinions. Second, you may lose control over the entire process if too many people become involved. To avoid these pitfalls, make sure you keep a tight grip on proceedings, and limit the number of opinions you seek to those that are really essential. When you involve others in your decision, explain the whole picture. Telling half a story can lead very quickly to rumors, with a subsequent drop in staff morale. Token or partial consultation does not succeed.

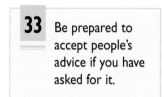

33 Be prepared to accept people's advice if you have asked for it.

34 Encourage people to participate in decisions to get better results.

LISTENING TO OTHERS

The manager who reverses a decision after hearing the contrary views of a meeting is strong rather than weak. Positive listening means not just hearing the words but understanding their significance and recognizing their sense. You do not want unthinking endorsement of your decisions. Encourage those you consult to speak their minds, and ensure that you have a representative spread of interests and perceptions. Advocate a background of continuous consultation, using every device you can, from team meetings to suggestion boxes. This will enable you to make decisions based on a real understanding of the attitudes of others. Remember that consulting others does not necessarily mean inviting endless debate. Seek views and information and listen to what is said, but decide on the best course of action yourself.

QUESTIONS TO ASK YOURSELF

Q Am I presenting my own view in the most rational, understandable way?

Q Am I changing my mind because of fluent argument, or is there a sound reason?

Q Have I ever ignored attempts to consult with me about a problem before?

Q Am I listening properly to others and hearing what they are really saying?

Q Do I give colleagues the chance to express their own opinions?

SOLICITING OPINIONS INFORMALLY ▼
To understand the opinions of your colleagues fully, it is important to built up a strong and open rapport. Take time away from the office to discuss matters informally and without constraint – the results will be honest and positive.

Reassure colleagues that you are speaking to them in confidence

Open body language shows colleagues feel at ease together

USING ANALYTICAL METHODS

To reach a sound decision, you need to analyze all the relevant facts. There are several analytical tools that are both useful and simple to employ. Use analysis to lead to strong conclusions, and therefore good strategic decision-making.

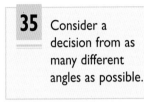

35 Consider a decision from as many different angles as possible.

36 Know your three largest rivals as intimately as your own company.

USING SWOT ANALYSIS ▼
The chart below highlights key questions to be asked. By identifying an organization's Strengths and Opportunities, and pinpointing its Weaknesses and Threats, effective strategies can be made for the future.

ANALYZING YOUR SWOT

SWOT analysis helps establish where an organization, team, or product stands in the marketplace. Your organization's SWOT – an acronym for Strengths, Weaknesses, Opportunities, and Threats – holds the key to future strategic decision-making. Make an honest and realistic list under the above headings. As you do, you may unearth valuable facts – often the analysis alone highlights areas that you may have overlooked – and realize that your organization's weaknesses may be as important as its strengths. Having analyzed your own SWOT, analyze that of your competitors.

UNDERSTANDING YOUR ORGANIZATION'S SWOT

STRENGTHS
What is the organization competent at? What is it really good at?

WEAKNESSES
Is the organization short of key resources or capabilities? Is it vulnerable to competition?

OPPORTUNITIES
Can the organization sell more, or find new markets, products, or services?

THREATS
Can the organization's products or technology be overtaken? Are its markets deteriorating?

RELATING PRICE TO QUALITY

A key decision is where to position a product in the market. Use a price/quality matrix to relate price to quality. If your ultimate aim is high price/high quality, you still may want to use another strategy initially, such as selling your product at medium price/medium quality, as a stepping stone to get there. If analysis shows that lower profit margins can be offset by winning a larger share of the market, you can still profit by selling top-quality products at medium or even low prices.

Organizations frequently aim at placing a high price/high quality product on the market

▲ USING THE PRICE/QUALITY MATRIX

This matrix shows that the rising quality of products can accompany a corresponding rise in price to give the best profit margins within the market. The matrix gives nine alternatives for positioning the overall stance of a product in the market.

COMBINING ANALYSES

A single piece of analysis may well need to be combined with other approaches to gain a view of the complete picture. Analysis ensures that you understand the problems and can safely make decisions that will markedly improve results. Combining different types of analysis is a way of strengthening the analysis – and the stronger it is, the stronger the pointers to the correct decision, and the better the chances of getting it right. For example, the price/quality matrix can be combined with a study of market growth rate and relative market share, or RMS. RMS represents sales as a percentage of the combined sales of your three largest rivals. The best RMS is 100 percent or more. If it is less, you should not reduce the high price of your high quality product to medium, because you do not have a large enough market share.

CULTURAL DIFFERENCES

The phenomenon of "paralysis by analysis" refers to an over-reliance on analysis in business situations that can lead to an inability to reach decisions. It does occur in the American business community, which can be obsessed with numbers. At the other extreme, the British have a tendency for inadequate analysis, while other Europeans fall between the two extremes. The Japanese are thorough analysts but avoid "paralysis" by acting fast once decisions are final.

GENERATING IDEAS

The creation of new ideas is vital to bringing fresh light to the decision-making process. When looking for ideas, try to achieve a balance between imagination and practicality. Your first hurdle lies in generating the ideas with others.

 37 Be disorganized when generating ideas, organized in developing them.

CHALLENGING TRADITIONS

When making decisions, do not blindly accept tried-and-tested "conventional wisdom." Try it yourself; be ruthless in its application and open-minded about alternatives. It is not wrong to use a conventional approach, but do so only after you have fully and fairly examined other new and more innovative ideas. Compare the obvious and easy with the unorthodox and difficult, and you may well find the latter the better solution by far .

 38 Promote lateral thinking, but try to develop ideas in a logical fashion.

BRAINSTORMING FOR IDEAS

Brainstorming meetings are held specifically to generate new ideas. Gather a group of people – three to eight ideally – and ask each to submit an idea (or list of ideas) relevant to the decision being made. As each idea is produced, the group facilitator should record it. Be democratic. Do not reject any ideas, and be sure to value a junior's idea as highly as that of a senior. The more ideas generated, the better, but do not judge or analyze them, or make any decisions, during the session.

▲ **ENCOURAGING PARTICIPATION**
New ideas help people to look outside the confines of their own jobs. Brainstorming is useful for breaking creative logjams, but you need more disciplined methods for actual decision-making.

PRODUCING NEW IDEAS

When setting up any group to generate ideas, choose the participants to reflect differences in expertise and experience. Define the issues and the relevant criteria clearly, and make sure that all ideas are recorded. It is useful to have a facilitator, who does not contribute ideas, to keep the session on course. Part of the facilitator's role is to promote lateral thinking. If a seemingly absurd proposition is offered, he or she should use it to provoke fresh thinking. When enough ideas have been presented, end the meeting. Select the ideas that are worthy of further investigation, and follow up promptly. You could use the same group of people to evaluate the analyses and advise on the best alternative.

 39 Be provocative if you feel that your team is too staid.

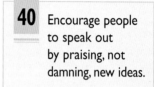 **40** Encourage people to speak out by praising, not damning, new ideas.

ENCOURAGING THE CREATIVE PROCESS

Generating a relaxed environment in which individuals feel comfortable and unthreatened helps to draw out new ideas. The more closely a set of people work together, the easier it is for them to relax and build up trust in one other.

If you are leading a meeting intended to generate new and creative policies, consider using some of the following methods:

- Ask all the attendees to come to the meeting prepared to present two or three ideas each.
- Give everybody at the meeting the chance to air their views in turn.
- Do not allow the creative flow of ideas to be ruined by imposing too many constraints or making assumptions.
- Do not allow interruptions or discussions to wander too far off the subject in

question, but encourage the free, creative flow of ideas and associations.

- Try asking your colleagues to circulate ideas in advance of the meeting – this may help those who like to work alone to develop their ideas.
- Provide the group with a few ideas of your own – this will help to direct discussions and act as stimulation if inspiration seems to be running dry.
- Try to encourage lateral thinking as well as logical thought to break down and challenge any long-held preconceptions.
- Put together all the ideas generated into clusters so that you end up with groups of related ideas. At this point, start to create a shortlist of the best ideas.
- Above all, never criticize any of the ideas in front of your colleagues.

DEVELOPING CREATIVE THINKING

There is a common misconception that creative thinking, and therefore the ability to make innovative decisions, is an inborn talent that cannot be learned. Try to develop the quality and originality of your ideas by adopting new methods of thinking.

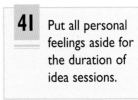

41 Put all personal feelings aside for the duration of idea sessions.

EMBRACING NEW IDEAS

People – and organizations – form habits of thinking just as they form other habits. Many organizations that reject new thinking outright do so because they view change as risk. There are, however, ways to defeat this negativity and encourage an acceptance of the new. For example, in any type of ideas meeting, forbid the use of the response "Yes, but..." – a classic idea killer – until a predetermined number of new ideas have been explored and discussed.

42 Make people think atypically, and they may come up with atypical ideas.

THINKING POSITIVELY

If you are cautious by nature, you are not very likely to think adventurously, but if you are highly creative, you may be impatient with skeptics who see only the objections in a discussion. Do not allow colleagues to get locked into these or any other mind-sets that prevent them from listening to other points of view with an open mind. If you think that a debate is becoming too negative, say so and ask everybody to try and make a positive, creative contribution. This will help you avoid sterile debates in which everyone defends their own fixed position and attacks all others.

43 Always encourage new, unexplored ways of thinking.

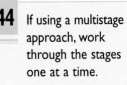

44 If using a multistage approach, work through the stages one at a time.

DECIDING ON ACTION

The object of generating new ideas is to find the best one and act on it. Expert Mark Brown uses a five-stage model (given the acronym AGISA) for the group thinking process. It starts with Analysis, in which you seek to uncover the issues affecting the decision. That enables you to set Goals – either "opportunities" (coded white) or "problems" (gray). Then you search for Ideas, which are either "conventional, mildly original" (light blue) or "unconventional, needing further discussion" (blue). At the Selection (red) stage, ideas are examined for weakness and solutions are discarded or adopted. Those adopted call for Action (green), in which the accepted decision is implemented.

POINTS TO REMEMBER

- Assumptions should always be challenged.
- Conventional thinking should not be rejected just because it is conventional.
- New ideas are as valuable as any others but should not be adopted simply because they are new.

▼ GATHERING IDEAS

In the AGISA thinking model, you must complete each stage of idea generation before moving on. In any given situation you may need to follow either one or both of the possible routes shown here.

ASSESSING THE VALIDITY OF IDEAS

After you have generated a range of ideas, you need to assess them. Apply objective criteria and use rational methods to narrow down the range of choices, and keep an open mind when deciding which ideas you want to take forward to the next stage.

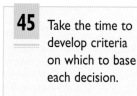

45 Take the time to develop criteria on which to base each decision.

46 Make sure that ideas are able to rise up your organization.

NARROWING THE OPTIONS

Use "What if?" analysis when the time comes to assess the value of ideas. Ask yourself what would be the likely consequences of adopting decision A, B, or C. Discuss and establish the answers in group debates that consider the situation from all angles. Make the most of these meetings by asking people to present their views one at a time rather than descending into a free-for-all debate.

OVERCOMING RIGID THINKING

There are several methods of overcoming rigid thinking. First, ensure that the structure of your organization will not inhibit the adoption of innovative ideas. Second, ask people to spend time thinking about ideas before meetings, and third, use multiskilled teams that cut across departmental boundaries to expose people to different disciplines and experience.

▼ **BEING OPEN-MINDED**
In this encounter, one person's defensive seated posture shows a defensive attitude toward his colleague's ideas.

Open posture

Defensive posture

LISTING THE ▶ OPTIONS

When assessing a range of new ideas, write down the problem, all suggested solutions, and the potential outcomes of each.

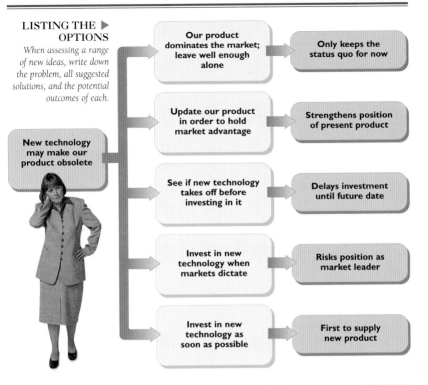

New technology may make our product obsolete

Options	Outcomes
Our product dominates the market; leave well enough alone	Only keeps the status quo for now
Update our product in order to hold market advantage	Strengthens position of present product
See if new technology takes off before investing in it	Delays investment until future date
Invest in new technology when markets dictate	Risks position as market leader
Invest in new technology as soon as possible	First to supply new product

NARROWING DOWN IDEAS

The best way to reduce a long list of options to a manageable size is to have clear criteria. For example, for an investment decision, the criteria could relate to the maximum investment, the payback period, the return on capital, and strategic fit. Having selected criteria, you can then safely discard ideas that fall outside them. If this type of test is unsuitable – for example, on recruitment issues – list the pros and cons of each alternative, and then attribute them with scores out of ten according to how great their affect is on each advantage. Discard the lowest scoring alternatives.

QUESTIONS TO ASK YOURSELF

Q How well do the alternatives fit the criteria?

Q What is the balance between the disadvantages and advantages of the solution?

Q What will be the consequences of each solution?

Q Have I canvassed all relevant views and opinions?

Q Do I know which solution has the widest support?

GATHERING INFORMATION

Once you have narrowed down all your ideas, you may need to research them in more detail in order to check out their viability and understand their implications. Think carefully about the questions you need to ask to evaluate the situation properly.

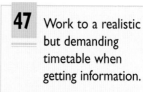

47 Work to a realistic but demanding timetable when getting information.

POINTS TO REMEMBER

● Your requirements should be assessed thoroughly before embarking on any research.

● The Internet provides an excellent source of all kinds of information and data.

● Using the wrong methodology for research will lead to the wrong results being produced.

● A clear, concise, and accurate interpretation of the data that you have acquired is the most crucial factor in its usage.

RESEARCHING PROPERLY

Vast amounts of information are now available from more sources than ever before. Focus your research by asking yourself what information you would ideally obtain in order to make your decision. Write down the contents of this "ideal information pack," and check how much is available and where. Stick to your ideal, and try to glean as much of it as possible, taking care not to exclude anything that is relevant. Sometimes, it can be easy to overlook important details that might sway your choice – especially if you are not being sufficiently objective.

UTILIZING RESOURCES

Start with your company's own resources. Look for data that has not been analyzed. One accountant found that toothpaste sales to pharmacies were far less profitable than those to chains. The outcome was a profit of millions. Consulting electronic media brings in a whole world of information, but printed media may be more accessible. The information industry has grown enormously, and consulting firms can give invaluable guidance, especially on competitive activity. Conferences and seminars are vital for networking, and be sure not to neglect your colleagues inside the company.

48 When delegating information-gathering, use your brightest people.

49 Do not throw away source material – you may find you need it later.

HANDLING INFORMATION

Before you feed information into the decision-making process, organize and check it thoroughly. Reports from outside consultants or internal sources should come properly organized, with all the conclusions clearly stated at the beginning of the report, supporting data arranged in a logical order, and all relevant information gathered into logical sections. Treat reports exactly like all other information – never take anything for granted. If the data comes from too small or unrepresentative a sample, or the questions were loaded, you will not be able to rely on the information. Can it be cross-checked? If so, do it. When satisfied, organize your research along similar lines to the consulting reports for consistency. Use this information as the basis for your decision and for any plan of action.

THINGS TO DO

1. Look out for interesting information, and file it away for future use.

2. Establish good relations with in-house librarians, finance departments, and other information sources.

3. Build your own library of reference books, press clippings, and reports.

4. Keep looking at the overall problems as well as the specific details when searching for material.

LOCATING INFORMATION

SOURCES	FACTORS TO CONSIDER
COMPANY RESOURCES Includes company library, internal statistics, finance department, colleagues, and researchers.	● A good starting point for most information-gathering. ● Can be time-consuming if much unwanted data must be searched through to find something relevant. ● Is dependent on cooperation of colleagues.
INDIVIDUAL SOURCES Includes friends, outside contacts, competitors, seminars, press reports, and publications.	● Useful ideas and contributions can come from people at any level of any business. ● Many informal, individual sources of information may be difficult to exploit fully.
EXPERTS Includes management and other consultants, market and economic research, and academic experts.	● Level of expertise should be high and broadly based. ● May take time for experts to find relevant information. ● Quality of the service is likely to be high, though proposals and references will need careful checking.
ELECTRONIC MEDIA Includes Internet, intranet, PC and other computer networks, and all on-line information services.	● The World Wide Web and other such services provide a wealth of useful information – perhaps too much. ● Global links are slow at busy times of the day. ● Information may not always be accessible or correct.

ASSESSING COMPETITION

Before implementing any decision, spend some time looking at how it will affect the market and what reactions it might cause among your competitors. It is essential to carry out extensive market research if you want to understand and counteract competitive activity. So, find out from your customers how they rate both your product and your competitors', and act on these findings. Another way to approach your competition is by applying what is known as "game theory."

50 Regularly research your market, and act on the results.

51 Keep information on the behavior of competitors.

KNOWING THE SYSTEM

According to game theory, an organization and its competitors all form part of the same "business system," which has boundaries, players, and a set of rules – all of which you must learn as you play. Also you must understand the key relationships between cause and effect. Any change in one part of the system will be reflected throughout it. Players in the game never make a decision without considering all foreseeable effects.

52 Understand the rules of the game, and change them to your advantage.

CHANGING THE RULES

Traditionally, beating the competition involved offering better goods or services, and doing so at lower costs. However, in today's marketplace, this has become much harder, and is not always possible. An alternative method is to change the rules of the game. To gain the advantage, think of how your products or services are currently being supplied, and look for radically different ways to reach the market – by selling directly to customers, or opening a 24-hour, seven-days-a-week "shop" on the Internet. To be a successful player, go for moves that other players either will not or cannot follow, and attack their weaknesses by developing and exploiting unique strengths of your own.

THINGS TO DO

1. Always be aware of exactly what your competition is doing in the marketplace.

2. Look for innovative, new ways to attract people to your product or service.

3. Keep one step ahead of the competition.

4. Once you have researched the market, change your sales policy as necessary.

FORMING ALLIANCES

In sports, opposing teams have common interests, such as getting the largest possible attendance at their games. Business players also have common interests – they may compete for market share, but they all want to maximize the total market. Look for organizations complementary to your own, and form alliances allowing you to play on the same side in one sector of the market, yet compete in others. Such supplier-customer alliances can mean improved performance and lower costs, with everyone sharing the benefits.

▲ WORKING TOGETHER
Competing sports teams have mutual interests. It is to their advantage to create as big a "market" as possible (in this case, spectators) to create revenue. Both sides strive to play a great game, thus pleasing their fans and increasing their market.

QUESTIONS TO ASK YOURSELF

Q Are there areas of common ground with our competitors?

Q How can we cooperate in each area of common ground?

Q Would our competitors benefit the most?

Q Would our company benefit the most?

Q How can we maintain competitive vigor?

53 Anticipate competitors' actions in order to compete successfully against them in the marketplace.

FORECASTING THE FUTURE

Decision-making rests on predicting the future and assuming that events will unfold following an established action plan. Develop methods of improving the accuracy of your own forecasts and ways of using forecasts made by others to best effect.

54 Consider all the criteria involved in making a decision before committing.

55 Check forecasts by your own intuition and experience.

56 Make the future happen – this is the most effective way of forecasting.

SELECTING METHODS

Most forecasting is based on extrapolation of figures. For example, when budgeting, you will look back at the costs and sales for the previous year, and base the estimates of the next year's sales and costs on the increases and decreases that you anticipate. This method of forecasting is also used as the basis for longer-term planning. As a more dynamic alternative, work back from the future: envisage your desired outcome, then plan the action required to achieve it. This is an exercise in creating, rather than merely predicting, the future, and is the key to making progressive, proactive decisions.

TAKING A WIDER VIEW

When making a forecast, you need to consider criteria both internally, within your organization, and externally, in the outside market. For instance, if you are proposing a full-scale program to develop a new product, you should forecast the following:

INTERNAL CONSIDERATIONS:
- Financial – how will you raise the cash?
- Structural – where will the operation be based?
- Staff – who will manage the operation?
- Development – how long will this take?
- Timing – at what time of year will the product be launched?

EXTERNAL CONSIDERATIONS:
- Customers – where is the market?
- Market – how strong will the market be at the launch date?
- Competitors – how will they react?
- Promotion – what will be required and how much will it cost?
- Investors – will you need more money?

QUESTIONS TO ASK YOURSELF

Q Am I aware of all the variables and alternatives involved in making this forecast?

Q Can I assess the likelihood of each possible outcome of my forecast?

Q Have I built any margin for error into my forecasting and, if so, is it realistic?

Q Am I making a rational assessment of all the possibilities?

Q Have I forgotten to include anything major that will have a serious effect on the forecast?

USING FORECASTS

The most important element in forecasting is judgment. Use your experience and intuition to estimate the value of predictions. Ask "what if" questions – "what happens if the sales forecast is raised by 50 percent?" – and treat the forecast as dynamic, updating it as information comes in. For example, revise your annual budget in the light of performance over the first quarter. In this way forecasting becomes a flexible tool for controlling, monitoring, and planning the future.

57 Question every assumption before making your forecast – and then check them again.

ASSESSING SUCCESS

The future rarely imitates the past exactly, so some degree of error is inevitable when making forecasts. Refine your forecast using "probability theory" to reduce the element of error. Assess the likelihood of an event occurring on a scale of 0 ("no chance") to 1 ("certain"), with a 50 percent chance of success scoring 0.5. For example, two potential investments are forecast to show profits of $20,000 and $40,000, rating 0.5 and 0.4. Multiplying outcomes by probabilities gives these figures: $20,000 x 0.5 = $10,000; $40,000 x 0.4 = $16,000. So, even with a lower probability of total success, the $40,000 project is clearly the better option.

▼ **FORECASTING TO WIN**
This company wanted to triple its market share within a specific time limit. The chief executive worked backward from this outcome to find out what steps were needed to achieve it. Strategists worked with forecasts to produce detailed plans that would turn ambition into reality.

CASE STUDY
A company selling its product at premium prices was hit by the introduction of low-priced competition. Forecasts confirmed that this trend would continue in a market showing strong growth. Extrapolating figures from its own results showed that the company would lose its market share and profit over a very short period of time.

The chief executive decided to look for a future in which the company became so competitive on costs and prices that it would triple its market share within four years.

To achieve this, the company planned a rise in production and sales figures. Working back from that high ambition, the strategists worked out the forecasts and targets for costs, margins, production, and the introduction of new products. With careful targeting, the chief executive's vision of a tripled market share was realized two years ahead of schedule.

USING MODELS

As a decision maker, you should become familiar with "modeling," such as simple spreadsheets or computer-generated graphics. Use these vital tools to test variables, test relationships between data, and predict the consequences of alteration in any factors.

58 Simulate and predict the future rather than waiting for it to happen.

USING COMPUTERS

Processes of any kind can be simulated mathematically to imitate real-life causes and effects. Many computer programs go beyond simple spreadsheets to explore and illustrate what would happen if certain decisions were made, and to anticipate the long-term effects of competitors' reactions. Ask an expert's advice on which program to use, and be sure that everybody working with it is properly trained. Good computer graphics are easy to access and understand, and forecasting in this way may save the pain of real-life trial and error. Decision-making in once-complex areas like distribution logistics and inventory control has now become routine with the advent of more and more powerful computer programs. These can quickly deal with complex calculations and produce user-friendly statistics.

▼ RAISING PRICES

This equation helps you decide if you can raise prices, by showing how far sales can fall before profitability declines. In this example where c equals 25, if the product price is raised by 20 percent, profits will not fall until sales drop by more than 44 percent (Critical Volume Loss), making this a risk worth taking.

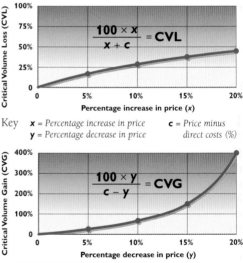

$$\frac{100 \times x}{x + c} = CVL$$

Key x = Percentage increase in price c = Price minus
  y = Percentage decrease in price   direct costs (%)

$$\frac{100 \times y}{c - y} = CVG$$

▲ LOWERING PRICES

This equation helps you decide if you can cut your product prices, by showing how far sales must rise at the new price in order to sustain profits. If the product price is dropped by 20 percent when c equals 25, sales must rise by 400 percent (Critical Volume Gain) to maintain profit levels. This is clearly not a viable strategy.

USING CONSULTANTS

Specialist techniques are best applied by specialists. If in-house resources are inadequate for a particular task, it makes sense to use outside consultants. There are many consulting firms with specific experience in highly refined forecasting, modeling, and computer simulation techniques – but such expertise does not come cheap. To make the most of this specialist knowledge, always provide a thorough brief.

GETTING HELP ▶
As a manager, you have to make decisions, some of which may be based on forecasts and models. To use time efficiently, hire consultants and provide them with a detailed brief of your modeling requirements.

HANDLING RESULTS

No matter how experienced the forecaster, his or her results can only be as good as the information they are given to work with. Bear in mind the acronym GIGO – "Garbage In, Garbage Out." Make sure that all relevant data is gathered as comprehensively and accurately as possible. If the results of modeling seem hard to believe, check the validity of any assumptions that have been made, and the methodology used, before acting on the forecasts. Never ignore disconcerting modeling results, however. You may well find that they have arisen because vital information has been overlooked, or important consequences have not been properly taken into account.

59 Do complex calculations yourself only if you have the skills.

60 If the model contradicts your beliefs, check and double-check.

MINIMIZING RISKS

Most decisions contain a degree of uncertainty. Use your own judgment and experience to remove as much doubt as possible from a situation. Think through the consequences of your actions, be prepared to compromise, and consider timing carefully.

61 Use both judgment and calculation to get the optimum value from each.

62 Never sacrifice the future for the short-term unless there is no option.

63 Make competitive decisions earlier rather than later.

ASSESSING CONSEQUENCES

Making a decision usually results in some form of action being taken at some point in the future. Minimize risks by listing the possible effects of any action, and assessing the likelihood of each negative event, as well as how much damage it could inflict. Also, assess consequences in terms of time – immediate, short term, or long term – and consider the long-term results of a decision rather than looking exclusively at short-term effects. Look for external factors that could affect your decision, and try to quantify the likelihood of – and reasons for – your plan failing. Itemizing such factors is a step toward making contingency plans to deal with any problems. This will reduce the chance of failure and optimize your chances of success.

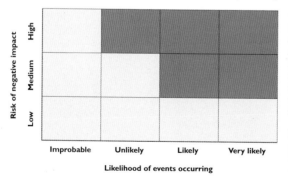

◀ **ASSESSING RISKS**
This matrix combines the chances of an event occurring with the severity of its impact on a decision. If it is very unlikely that an event may occur, a high risk of negative impact may be sustainable. A very likely to occur/high negative impact result needs rethinking.

Key
■ *High risk of negative impact*
□ *Low risk of negative impact*

USING TRADE-OFFS

Successful management involves many trade-offs and compromises to reach the best decision when several factors are involved. The aim of trade-offs is to keep short- and long-term risks as low as possible. You cannot maximize profits and investment at the same time – short-term profit is sacrificed in favor of long-term success. Equally, ambitious plans for expansion may be trimmed to achieve satisfactory current returns. Products are similarly affected – you cannot simultaneously maximize a car's acceleration and minimize its fuel usage.

To make decisions satisfactorily, work out your priorities and assess those of your opposition. Establish which features matter most to customers to compile an order of priorities – you can then trade off the less important features against the significant ones. Although some trade-offs involve reducing costs, few customers will be willing to accept the sacrifice of quality to profit.

TIMING IMPLEMENTATION

Many projects fail because their timing is wrong – they start too early or too late. When dealing with the launch of a new product, for example, a trade-off may be needed between having all the necessary elements securely in place and moving swiftly in order to beat your competitors to the market. Although the latter seems the riskier alternative, you may lose out to the competition altogether if you delay for too long. Have the confidence to decide and implement quickly, and delay only if there are convincing reasons for waiting.

▼ PLANNING AHEAD
Use wall charts that show all information relating to a decision to help you plan your time well in advance and to calculate the optimum time for implementing a decision.

USING FAIL-SAFE STRATEGIES

*D*ecision makers need to take a broad view and consider the impact of different outcomes. Having assessed the risks, try to build in safety nets to minimize them. This will enable you either to succeed in full confidence or fail in relative safety.

65 Never make a rash decision – it is much less likely to be successful.

66 Planning specialists may be more valuable as critics than as planners.

PLANNING SCENARIOS

When assessing the potential risks involved in a decision, always ask yourself "What is the best combination of consequences ("best case") that I can reasonably expect from the decision? And the worst ("worst case")?" The key word here is "reasonably." Neither optimism or pessimism should be taken to extremes, but this simplest form of scenario-planning shows whether the "best case" payoff justifies taking "worst case" risks.

▼ **CHOOSING A STRATEGY**
Of the three outcomes shown below, the "best case" scenario is the outcome to be hoped for, but considering alternatives and preparing to meet all eventualities allows contingency plans to be made.

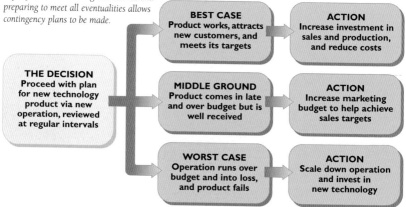

THE DECISION
Proceed with plan for new technology product via new operation, reviewed at regular intervals

BEST CASE
Product works, attracts new customers, and meets its targets

ACTION
Increase investment in sales and production, and reduce costs

MIDDLE GROUND
Product comes in late and over budget but is well received

ACTION
Increase marketing budget to help achieve sales targets

WORST CASE
Operation runs over budget and into loss, and product fails

ACTION
Scale down operation and invest in new technology

POINTS TO REMEMBER

- Differences should never just be split between best and worst case scenarios – there is always middle ground to be found.

- Big risks should not be taken if the rewards are small.

- While planning for the best, it is important to be prepared for the worst.

- A broad range of people should take part in scenario-planning.

- If none of the scenarios seems attractive, there should be a major rethinking of ideas.

DEVELOPING SCENARIOS

So-called "single-point forecasts" that predict only one eventuality are more risky than plans that consider a range of possible outcomes. Work out alternative scenarios for yourself, filling in as much detail as possible, so that you are better prepared for actual events. For example, you could forecast prices in your industry on the basis of increases by competitors, no change, or price cuts. The three alternatives will lead to three alternative strategies. Pick the strategy that best fits the scenarios as a whole, or select as your goal the most attractive scenario outcome and make decisions that optimize your chances of reaching that target.

DISCUSSING ALTERNATIVES

Producing scenarios is an ideal way of bringing colleagues into the decision-making process. You can examine key questions objectively and use the answers to react effectively when the situation occurs in real life. What are the main variables? What happens to them in each scenario? Are assumptions or subjective thinking affecting the issue? What are your best responses if and when a particular scenario materializes?

67 Check any action plans against the desired outcome.

TALKING ▶ FREELY
Discuss a variety of scenarios with colleagues, and consider all options before you move toward consensus for a final decision.

Colleague requests more detail of various plans of action

Leader outlines potential outcomes

Colleague wants to make an informed decision

ASSESSING THE CONSEQUENCES FOR STAFF

While assessing ideas in order to make a decision, consider the options for your staff. They may feel unhappy about imminent change if they are not consulted, or if you need to recruit new people with the necessary skills to implement your decision.

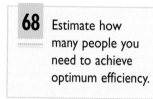

68 Estimate how many people you need to achieve optimum efficiency.

69 Ensure that staff have access to information whenever possible.

ASSESSING REQUIREMENTS

Most decisions made within an organization will have consequences for existing staff. Once you have made a decision, consider the number of people required to execute it with optimum efficiency. In addition, decide which skills are needed to fulfill the plan, and at what stages of the plan they will be deployed. Always inform existing staff of decisions made on recruitment issues, which are often highly sensitive. If you do need to recruit new skills, explain your reasons, basing them on your objectives and action plan.

REVIEWING STAFF SKILLS

Examine the strengths and weaknesses of the existing workforce before making a final decision on their deployment. You may find that their numbers and skills match exactly those required by your decision and any subsequent plan of action. However, it is much more likely that you will need to change some roles or give some people more responsibility. There may be overlap in responsibility, and some people may no longer be needed. Others may require specialist training to upgrade or augment their skills.

70 Consider existing skills when deciding future action.

71 Be objective when making staffing decisions.

REDEPLOYING PEOPLE

There will often be quite a considerable degree of emotional resistance among staff if your decision demands substantial recruitment of new people, reorganization, changing roles, or losing roles altogether. Keep staff informed, and consult them at every stage of the decision-making process so that they will be better prepared for the outcome. The impact of redeploying people or them experiencing job loss, however, can still be traumatic and will require diplomatic handling. Take care to explain all the reasons if you have to replace existing staff, and handle any necessary layoffs with generosity, tact, and sympathy – especially over money matters.

▼ DISCUSSING ROLES
When discussing role changes with staff, always be honest yet tactful. Prepare for the meeting by noting down possible responses to their objections to help you deal with them calmly and diplomatically.

Manager anticipates objections and lists some solutions

INVOLVING A NEW TEAM

Once a new team is in place, act swiftly to involve people fully in making your decision effective. See that everybody has a concise job description and knows exactly how they fit into the team. Give new recruits an introduction to your organization, and ensure that they are quickly integrated into the team. Explain both the reasons that led to your decision and the action required to implement it clearly so that everybody knows the common aims. Provide stretching goals to encourage team members to work hard toward fulfilling these aims and executing your decision.

QUESTIONS TO ASK YOURSELF

Q What qualities do I want in the staff who will help to implement my decisions?

Q What qualities are already available in the people I can call upon?

Q Will I need to recruit more people with fresh skills to cover the tasks required?

Q Have I told existing staff I may have to recruit new skills?

MAKING YOUR DECISION

When your preparations are completed and the moment of decision finally arrives, double-check that you are making the right decision. Reassess your options and seek other opinions to reinforce your point of view. Once you are fully convinced, go ahead.

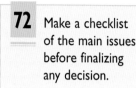

72 Make a checklist of the main issues before finalizing any decision.

QUESTIONS TO ASK YOURSELF

Q How likely am I to change my mind if given more time or information?

Q Has the decision-making process been thorough and sensible?

Q Have other minds made a large enough contribution to this decision?

Q Am I pleased and happy with this decision?

ASSESSING A DECISION

You have taken all possible care and every reasonable step to ensure that the decision is correct. Now, the die must be cast. Somebody must be hired or fired. An order will be placed, or a supplier dropped. An advertising campaign will be approved or rejected. Before setting action in motion, take time out to run over and assess the decision. What will it achieve? Why make it now? Will it be understood? How will it be received? The object is not to raise doubts in your mind, but to make yourself confident that a rational process has reached a reasonable decision.

ESTABLISHING YOUR COMMITMENT

In very rare cases, you may wish to avoid making what appears to be the best decision because you suspect that the action involved may expose you to risk and blame. This is avoiding responsibility, and may well do more harm than any personal risk involved in going ahead with a plan. When making a decision, ask yourself whether you are really committed to it, are prepared to take full responsibility for your actions, and are ready to face the consequences if you are proven to be wrong in the long term. Go ahead only if you can give a positive answer to all three questions.

73 Note that over-cautious decisions may stem from self-protection.

74 Try to uncover any hidden flaws before finalizing your decision.

REINFORCING DECISIONS

The most confident solo performer needs the comfort of talking through what they have decided, or are deciding, to do. Even when your mind is made up, it helps to talk over your final decision with a colleague or friend. Such a discussion, assuming that it is supportive, eases the stress of making the decision and provides another opportunity to go over the process, the pros and cons, and the reason for your choice. If in the course of discussion you uncover a vital flaw in the decision, so much the better. You can amend your decision while there is still time.

DEALING WITH DOUBT

The greatest single fear is that of getting it wrong. This is often combined with fear about the consequences for your job, your reputation, and your rewards. Do not bury such fears. Accept that every decision in life has a chance of error and that no individual or organization can make progress by being negative. Your fear of making a mistake can be eliminated completely only if you never make a decision at all. Instead of falling into this trap, take positive steps to strengthen your confidence. Remind yourself of what the worst case scenario is, assess what the chances are of the worst happening, and what the impact of this outcome would be. If you decide you can live with even the worst result, what is there to fear?

▲ AIRING OPINIONS INFORMALLY

An informal chat with a close colleague is one way of helping you over the stress of the decision-making process – and there is always a chance that they may uncover a flawed area that needs more work.

75 Write down all your predecision fears on paper, then throw them in the trash.

GETTING APPROVAL FOR YOUR FINAL DECISION

Once you have made your decision, it may need official sanction. If your superiors are fully informed of your progress, this may come readily. If not, try producing a written report or presentation – this can be a vital tool in gaining a positive response.

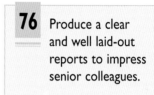

76 Produce a clear and well laid-out reports to impress senior colleagues.

77 Find a sponsor to improve chances of gaining approval for your decision.

OBTAINING APPROVAL

The fewer approvals required, the easier and better for the decision maker. The ideal is a one-stop approval; always try to limit the number of approval stages involved. However, in multi-layered hierarchies, with managers at each level needing to approve lower-level decisions, the decision-making process can be slow andeven frustrating. Employ patience and persistence to win the day.

PREPARING A REPORT

To proceed with some decisions, you may need to prepare a report detailing your recommendation and how you reached it. To be convincing, reports should state the following clearly:
- Why the decision is required;
- What action is recommended;
- How the action will be implemented;
- Who will be involved;
- When the action will happen.

Provide all the answers to these questions in a forceful opening summary, preferably on a single sheet of paper. Prepare the report as if you were writing a newspaper story – try using arresting headlines and bold type to emphasize key points.

THINGS TO DO

1. Always look at your decision hypercritically.
2. To make sure you have covered everything, go over your objectives again before starting your report.
3. List all the benefits reaped from your decision – as well as all the negatives.
4. Name the deadline when approval is required.

PROVIDING EVIDENCE

The single page summarizing your decision and its rationale should be supported by the data that has led to your conclusion. Think about who will read your report, and anticipate the questions they may ask, including some that are nit-picking and even obtuse. Remember that you have lived with this issue for some time, while other people are starting from scratch. Resist the temptation to cram the report so full of facts that readers will give up. Instead, provide the significant data organized in the same logical order as the summary.

78 Regard hostile questioning as a technique, not a personal attack.

PRESENTING YOUR IDEAS

If you have to present or explain your report in person, prepare for the meeting as for a major speech. Go over your material carefully and be prepared for counterattacks. Your seniors may believe that a "trial by fire" tests a team leader's case by teasing out any flaws. Even if your decision is subjected to brutal questioning, keep your cool and reaffirm your belief in your proposals. Remember that you have given great thought to this issue from all angles and have reached the best possible decision in the circumstances.

Open body language is used to instill confidence in a decision

◀ MAKING A PRESENTATION
Use visual aids to support your report, incorporating clear, good-quality diagrams as required. They may help win approval for a decision more quickly.

79 Ensure that you have covered all objections.

IMPLEMENTING A DECISION

Decisions are valueless until they are translated into positive action, which in turn involves the decision maker in making a series of operational decisions and choices.

DEVELOPING A PLAN

A plan of action will begin to evolve naturally as options are narrowed and their feasibility is studied during the decision-making process. Once you have made your final decision, concentrate on developing plans for its implementation.

80 Be sure of your decision before beginning to plan a course of action.

MAKING AN ACTION PLAN

When developing a plan to implement your decision, involve others in the plan. Use those with relevant abilities. Make sure that everybody fully understands the decision and the reasons for it. With their help, analyze the overall task, determine what actions should be taken, and decide when to implement the decision. Every activity should have start and stop dates, milestones for key events, and specified outcomes. The plan also specifies break points at which action can be reviewed and revised.

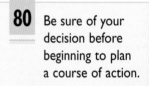

DELEGATING ACTION

Implementing some decisions – such as arranging meetings – can be handled by one person. More complex decisions, such as the creation of an advertising campaign or the launch of a new product, involves a number of tasks and the work of a team. Break these tasks into manageable chunks and delegate responsibility for planning each one to individuals within the team. Give these individuals freedom to act independently, and hold them personally accountable for their delegated activity. Remember that they are also responsible for their contribution to achieving the overall purpose of the decision. Your job is to ensure that accountability is clear and monitored, and that people are managed in a supportive way.

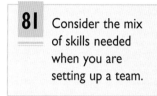

81 Consider the mix of skills needed when you are setting up a team.

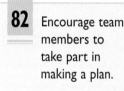

82 Encourage team members to take part in making a plan.

▼ BRIEFING A TEAM
When explaining a decision to the chosen team, find a visual way, if possible, to explain the context in which the decision was made and what will make it effective.

Team member raises a point

Leader explains decision

SETTING UP A PROJECT TEAM

In organizing a project team you must provide for all technical needs and cover all activities. Include team members in setting up; this will produce better plans and will also foster team spirit. As decision maker you will probably continue in the roles of coordinating all activities and building the team. Your functions will include ensuring that shared values are developed and that the team swiftly finds the best way of working as a group – from the first team meeting onward. You must also think about the roles the individual members will play. Make sure that everybody contributes to teamworking.

COMMUNICATING A DECISION

Once a decision is made and planned, relay it to those colleagues who need to know. Listen and respond to the reactions of staff at all levels, and keep everybody as closely involved as possible with your decision to avoid potential resistance.

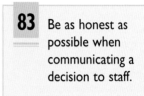

83 Be as honest as possible when communicating a decision to staff.

CLARIFYING A DECISION FOR COLLEAGUES

> **Break down your decision into its component parts**

> **Discuss the key objectives of each part of the decision**

> **Explain the actions required to complete each objective**

> **Delegate responsibility for completion of each action**

> **Give colleagues the deadline for completing each action**

> **Agree on points to monitor the progress of each action**

RELEASING INFORMATION

The release of information to everybody concerned in the implementation of a decision is part of the decision-making procedure. When done properly, it ensures that people understand exactly what has been decided and why, and it encourages their support. When you make your decision, explain which alternative action you have considered and the reason why you opted for your choice. Specify what the effects of your decision will be upon individuals. Be open to questioning, and try to remove doubts by making changes in response to genuine objections and concerns. Welcome contributions from anybody who will be affected.

MAINTAINING CONTACT

It is vital to keep everybody informed of progress as well as of changes in policy at all stages of the implementation of a decision. Team meetings, whether formal or informal, are ideal situations in which to discuss work-related problems, brainstorm new solutions to specific aspects of a decision, and air any general grievances. Encourage staff to speak to you in confidence about any interpersonal problems they may have, and, where appropriate, take action on their behalf.

AVOIDING SECRECY

When communicating a decision, lean toward releasing rather than suppressing information – and toward telling everyone involved, not just a chosen few. In traditional hierarchies, decisions are often reached behind closed doors, with the result that rumors may abound. This creates anxiety and uncertainty, and it lowers morale. Sometimes it may be necessary to keep good news under wraps, perhaps for reasons of security, but delaying bad news, understandable though it is, is always counterproductive. If you need to delay the release of information for any good reason, tell people when you expect to be able to give them details.

84 Spot check a few individuals within your organization to ensure that everyone has the right message.

SELLING DECISIONS

To "sell" your decision to colleagues who are not convinced of its viability you will need to:
● Ensure that you understand the needs of your colleagues;
● Present your decision in a way that matches these needs;
● Stress the advantages of the decision to the organization and individuals involved;
● Let colleagues do most of the talking, and try to turn all objections in your favor;
● Try to convince colleagues that they would have made the same decision as you when closing your "sale."

LETTING OTHERS KNOW OF YOUR DECISION

DECISION MAKER
As a decision maker, you need to inform colleagues throughout the organization of your decision and the actions required to fulfill it. You should use different approaches for different levels of staff.

INFORMING SUPERIORS
You may need to sell your decision to your superiors, since they usually have the ultimate power of veto over any course of action.

INFORMING COLLEAGUES
You may need to work to gain the support and trust of your colleagues, especially if they are suspicious of your motives.

INFORMING JUNIOR STAFF
You may need junior staff to help implement your decision, so invite them to contribute any specialized knowledge they have.

DISCUSSING THE PROGRESS OF A DECISION

Many meetings have no purpose but to discuss and inform. Some, however, are held specifically to discuss progress in the implementation of a decision. For the best results, be clear about what is expected from such meetings and who should attend.

85 As chairperson, control a meeting and do not become sidetracked.

86 Make sure the agenda for every meeting is clear to everyone present.

AVOIDING TIME-WASTING

It is important to avoid time-wasting when meeting to discuss the implementation of a decision. Prepare yourself by anticipating and obtaining all the facts that you require. Do you need to provide further evidence of the validity of your plans? Send the agenda, and any supporting papers, to participants in advance so that they can familiarize themselves with the issues. If any vital personnel are unable to attend, consider using telephone or video-conferencing facilities to provide a linkup.

CONDUCTING A MEETING

Keep a tight rein on the proceedings of meetings called to discuss any points raised or problems arising during the implementation of your decision. Make sure that each issue is properly tackled and that all the relevant data concerning your decision are included in the discussion. If necessary, you should guide the participants toward a consensus decision on how to improve an action plan. Try to streamline working procedures and to involve all those present at the meeting. Avoid arguments at all costs – they waste time that would be better spent in discussing and resolving the issues.

POINTS TO REMEMBER

- The fewer people who attend a meeting, the better.
- Agendas should be distributed as far in advance of a meeting as possible.
- Any new information to be provided in a meeting should be prepared well and presented as briefly as possible.
- Each person at a meeting must be given the chance to express their views; otherwise, there is no point in their being present.

FOLLOW-UP MEETINGS

Decisions taken at progress meetings should result in an action agenda, with designated people held responsible for seeing that the agenda is kept. Follow-up meetings are as important as the original discussions and must be treated as such. Each action should have a deadline attached, and the chairperson or a delegate should take charge of seeing that target dates are kept. If you are holding a series of meetings on a project, the action agenda should be reviewed at each meeting. Discrepancies, variances, and delays should be explained and any consequent decisions taken. The follow-up may indicate a need for radical change to the original decision or decisions. Do not hesitate to act accordingly.

DO'S & DON'TS

✔ Do produce an agenda laying out decisions to be reached in a meeting.

✔ Do make a note of who is following up each course of action.

✔ Do review any action planned at a meeting.

✔ Do face up to change if it proves necessary.

✘ Don't ignore what your team members have to say.

✘ Don't let deadlines drift – keep a tight rein on them.

✘ Don't neglect to prepare properly for each meeting.

✘ Don't be afraid to change your mind.

87 Always take into account the individual skills and personalities in the team you choose for action.

▼ DISCUSSING PLANS OF ACTION

Use meetings to discuss any problems that have occurred during the implementation of a decision. Monitor failure, but focus mainly on receiving constructive input from each participant and discussing improvements to future action plans.

Team member listens to new idea

Chairperson listens to comments by participant

Participant has new idea for solving problem

OVERCOMING OBJECTIONS

Decisions are likely to attract varying degrees of opposition, from mild dissent to outright resistance. Rather than feeling aggrieved, view opposition as a valuable part of decision-making, and respond with intelligence and care.

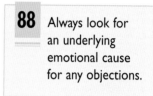

88 Always look for an underlying emotional cause for any objections.

LISTENING TO OBJECTIONS

Even if you need to push a decision through, never simply ignore objections or brush them aside – this is guaranteed to let misunderstanding fester. If you feel that those raising objections do not understand your position, remember it is likely that you do not fully understand theirs. Talk to people honestly, one to one, to find out what their complaints are – and the underlying causes. Having decided to reduce staff from 60 to 15, one boss asked those remaining for their views on the issue. It transpired that, although they had agreed with the decision in principle, they feared further dismissals. The boss reassured them that they were good workers, and indispensable. As a result of this two-way openness, morale improved and resentment ended.

89 Do not be belligerent – it is counterproductive.

▼ SPOTTING SIGNALS

It is crucial to observe and act on non-verbal signals. Recognizing resistance, doubt, or even cool appraisal can help you tackle objections in the best way.

Arms crossed defensively show lack of willingness

Face-cupping shows need for reassurance

RESISTANCE

DOUBT

Hand on chin shows appraisal is unemotional

Open, direct gaze indicates desire to be helpful

ASSESSMENT

SUPPORT

▲ **DELIVERING NEWS**
Whether the news is good or bad, tell it swiftly to forestall rumors and to canvass support. Create a relaxed atmosphere where people feel that you are willing to listen to any reservations they may have.

90 Involve your colleagues in any decision-making as much as possible.

RESPONDING TO STAFF

If you feel that a decision has raised a number of objections among the workforce, call a meeting to talk about the issues and clear the air. Even where a decision is final, and will be implemented, allow people to air their views freely, and listen carefully to what they have to say. You can often overcome opposition simply through listening, discussing, and reassuring. Your first need is to establish any specific complaints. Are the objections specific, and can they be removed by acceptable changes? If so, inform colleagues that these changes will be made.

FOCUSING ON BENEFITS

Sometimes a decision involves making changes that will have a negative impact on some staff. For example, if you are combining two departments, roles may change or become redundant. Reassure those affected that they are valued, either verbally or through financial compensation. To avoid hard feelings, explain fully why the decision was made. Outline the harm of maintaining an inefficient status quo, and always be positive as you describe the long-term benefits that the decision will bring.

POINTS TO REMEMBER

● People are most likely to accept unpleasant decisions when facts are presented in a positive light.

● If people feel able to come forward with objections, they tend to do so calmly.

● Irate people may make reasonable points that deserve answers.

● Even final decisions can be modified if there is good reason.

MONITORING PROGRESS

After a decision has been put into action, plans rarely go smoothly. There are usually unforeseen eventualities, such as poor performance from key people. Monitor progress to make sure you spot problems and can devise effective remedies.

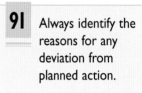

91 Always identify the reasons for any deviation from planned action.

92 If you overturn a subordinate's decision, explain the reasons for doing so.

MEASURING PROGRESS

The progress of an action plan based on your decision can be measured in time and cost. To monitor financial performance, compare actual expenditure with the budget. Accompany this with an updated forecast of final costs and of any revenue being generated. Set up an annual progress chart mapping the actual performance of the project, and compare this with the original plan to see where problems are arising. If you need to modify a plan, record in a log any changes, why they were made, who authorized them, and the outcome.

SELECTING BREAKPOINTS

You need to check progress of a project regularly, either at natural breakpoints or at specific intervals, to see whether your initial decision still holds good. This is particularly necessary when a decision affects a whole project. Drastic action may be required to put the project back on course, with parts or all of the action plan changing. Always make contingency plans in case the project needs to be abandoned – for example, if a business plan has weakened or staff performance is inadequate. Consider taking a "Go/No-Go" decision at selected breakpoints – for example, when research into the validity of a decision is completed or when the project has reached prototype stage.

POINTS TO REMEMBER

- Action agendas should be distributed to everyone who needs them.

- No-go decisions should mean starting again from scratch.

- Making the "best of a bad job", rather than giving up on an entire project, can sometimes be a wise decision.

- A subordinate's decision should be countermanded only if there is no alternative.

- Monitoring progress involves looking at implementation from several different angles.

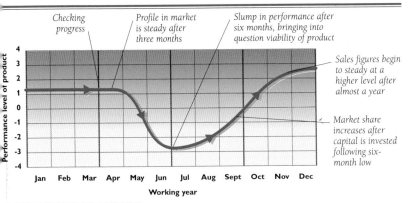

Checking progress

Profile in market is steady after three months

Slump in performance after six months, bringing into question viability of product

Sales figures begin to steady at a higher level after almost a year

Market share increases after capital is invested following six-month low

Performance level of product (y-axis: 4, 3, 2, 1, 0, -1, -2, -3, -4)

Jan Feb Mar Apr May Jun Jul Aug Sept Oct Nov Dec

Working year

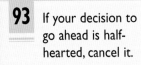

▲ WATCHING PROGRESS
This bar chart shows the progress of a new product in the marketplace. Since the performance was monitored and reviewed every three months, the dip in sales at six months was easily rectifiable – a further decision was taken to inject more capital.

93 If your decision to go ahead is half-hearted, cancel it.

MODIFYING DECISIONS

When reviewing decisions, ask yourself: "With the benefit of hindsight, would I make the same decision again?" If the answer is "No," review your decision and change the elements that are at fault. This may mean investing further capital or changing personnel. One manager launched a new product on the basis of market information that proved inaccurate. After a progress review, the product concept was radically altered and the staff in charge replaced – with great success.

OVERTURNING DECISIONS

Monitoring progress may spotlight decisions that are working badly or have been overtaken by events. If you find yourself obliged to overturn a decision made by somebody else, tread carefully. Be diplomatic, but remember that you need to put the good of an organization and the welfare of its people first. If a decision threatens the future or financial status of an organization or its people, react at once. Speak to all the people involved in implementing the original decision. If you are unable to find a way of solving the problem, consider restarting the whole process from scratch.

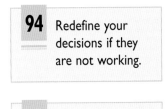

94 Redefine your decisions if they are not working.

95 Record all changes if you deviate at all from the agreed plan.

HANDLING OTHER PEOPLE'S DECISIONS

Decision-making can take a variety of forms – you may be given total responsibility for deciding on a plan and implementing it, or need to help with the decision of a superior. In each case, clarify the details of the problem under consideration.

96 Do not provide your delegator with too many report updates.

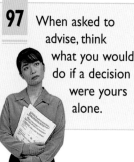

97 When asked to advise, think what you would do if a decision were yours alone.

COPING WITH DELEGATION

If a superior delegates a decision to you, you need to know whether you have total responsibility or whether the delegator wants to retain the ultimate power of approval. If delegation is total, you are required to keep the delegator informed only on a "need-to-know" basis, both for the decision process and on its implementation. If the delegator interferes heavily, either obey unquestioningly or try your powers of argument and diplomacy to do things your way. Consider the delegator's personality in order to judge which course of action is best.

MAKING A CONTRIBUTION

If you are invited to help a decision maker, you may be required to draw up a scenario, consider competitive response, explore technical limitations and opportunities, and so on. Remember that your mission is to assist rather than usurp, but take full advantage of the opportunity to influence the decision in whatever way you think is best. State your opinion without fear or favor: pulling punches does not help anyone. Do not be tempted to trim your views to fit those of the decision makers – you will be letting everybody down.

POINTS TO REMEMBER

● You need to understand every aspect of a problem if you are being asked to advise on the best way to solve it.

● Outside advisers should be providing helpful solutions rather than seeking to contradict.

● If it is difficult to agree fully with a decision, the use of tact and honesty is more helpful than a silent submission.

SEEKING CLARIFICATION

It is vital to be clear about any task delegated to you. If you are not sure that you have fully understood your boss at the briefing, note down any points needing clarification. Whether the reason is a failure to convey the brief clearly on the boss's part or simply that there is a lot of information to process at once, you must seek to clarify unanswered questions. Do not seek clarification too often; gather all the points on which you are unclear, and request one session to clear them all up.

Delegate queries points on written brief

▲ **UNDERSTANDING A BRIEF**
If you have received an unclear brief for a task, it is acceptable to ask your boss to write down exactly what is expected of you. Otherwise, you may fail to produce the desired result.

DO'S AND DON'TS

✔ Do question a superior's decision if it seems wrong.	✘ Don't try to take over a superior's decision.
✔ Do keep asking questions until you understand the brief.	✘ Don't just accept a decision for the sake of keeping the peace.
✔ Do feed back your understanding to any colleagues involved in carrying out the brief.	✘ Don't forget that decisions need to be "sold" to the people making the ultimate decisions for you.
✔ Do protest politely if interference from above is excessive.	✘ Don't forget your responsibilities to those working with you.

98 Gain an understanding of every detail of the brief so that you can carry out your task successfully.

UNDERSTANDING ACCOUNTABILITY

To carry out a task successfully, check what you are accountable for. What are you expected to do, how, and by when? To enable you to monitor and execute your task satisfactorily, devise your own action plan. However, there is a wider issue of responsibility – sticking to your accountable requirements may not be enough. Think carefully about your relationship with other people and other tasks, and keep these shared goals firmly in mind. Your aim should be to deliver a small success as part of a wider, overall success.

BUILDING ON DECISIONS

Few decisions stand completely alone. In most cases, one decision leads to others, forming a continuing process of feedback and analysis. To build successfully on a decision, learn your lessons from previously successful (and unsuccessful) plans of action.

99 Always be prepared for unexpected events to affect your plans.

100 Limit the number of your goals to keep them clear.

101 Be prepared to change your plan of action to suit new circumstances.

REVISING OBJECTIVES

At regular intervals, check that decisions are being made with final goals in mind. Are the original goals still valid? If so, which new decision can you take to augment those original aims? If not, revise your objectives and think again. For example, if you decide to sell a product direct to retailers, bypassing the wholesale trade, reaction from the middlemen may be bad, threatening heavy loss of business. Do you retreat, or seek a compromise with the wholesalers? You must decide how best to react to overall objectives.

Recording observations is crucial

PRIORITIZING DECISIONS

Do not delay badly needed decisions while you wait for the annual budget or the planning round. The regular budget and planning cycles cannot allow for the unexpected, such as the appearance of a revolutionary new product serving the same purpose as your own, but in a more effective way. Recognize that a disruptive event like this will demand radical steps outside the normal, predictable procedures of budgeting and planning. In this case, priority may be given to combating the revolutionary technology with major new investment, starting immediately, even though neither budget nor plan allow for the new strategy.

BUILDING ON SUCCESS

Postmortems in management, like those in medicine, usually follow disasters, while success is often neglected. However, it is always as important to know why a decision has succeeded as it is to explain a failure. The exact circumstances of the decision and its action plan may never recur, but a successful methodology could hold important lessons for use in the future. An "action review" technique, such as that employed by the US Army, is helpful. After every decision is implemented, sit down and review what went right and what went wrong, and why. Do not leave it at that. Record the lessons so that they can be absorbed and applied by others – and by you – in the future.

▼ REVIEWING AN ACTION PLAN

Use meetings to review action plans. Look at both positive and negative aspects of a situation so that successful outcomes can be repeated and any problems ironed out for the next time.

ASSESSING A DECISION'S EFFECTIVENESS

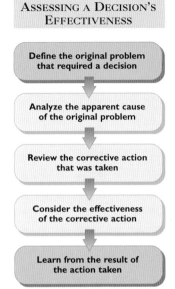

Define the original problem that required a decision

⬇

Analyze the apparent cause of the original problem

⬇

Review the corrective action that was taken

⬇

Consider the effectiveness of the corrective action

⬇

Learn from the result of the action taken

Active listening encourages participation

Giving positive feedback improves morale

ASSESSING YOUR ABILITY

Making the right decision every single time is practically impossible. However, employing the right processes, techniques, and tools can improve your chances of making the correct choices. Use the following self-assessment to test your decision-making abilities. Be as honest as you can: if your answer is "never," mark Option 1; if it is "always," mark Option 4; and so on. Add your scores together, then refer to the Analysis to see how you scored. Use your answers to identify the areas that need improving.

OPTIONS
1 Never
2 Occasionally
3 Frequently
4 Always

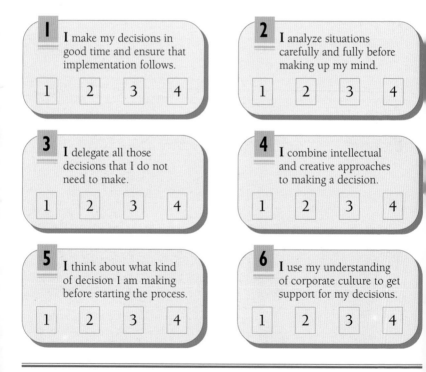

1 I make my decisions in good time and ensure that implementation follows.

1 | 2 | 3 | 4

2 I analyze situations carefully and fully before making up my mind.

1 | 2 | 3 | 4

3 I delegate all those decisions that I do not need to make.

1 | 2 | 3 | 4

4 I combine intellectual and creative approaches to making a decision.

1 | 2 | 3 | 4

5 I think about what kind of decision I am making before starting the process.

1 | 2 | 3 | 4

6 I use my understanding of corporate culture to get support for my decisions.

1 | 2 | 3 | 4

7 I prioritize significant factors according to the "20/80" rule.

| 1 | 2 | 3 | 4 |

8 I draw up a strong case to clarify and support any strategic decisions.

| 1 | 2 | 3 | 4 |

9 I seek the widest possible involvement in the decision-making process.

| 1 | 2 | 3 | 4 |

10 I consult all appropriate people to get their help in reaching the right decision.

| 1 | 2 | 3 | 4 |

11 I conduct SWOT analyses on my own – and competitors' – operations.

| 1 | 2 | 3 | 4 |

12 I root out obsolete ideas by taking a challenging and creative approach.

| 1 | 2 | 3 | 4 |

13 I encourage teams to think as a group – not as prejudiced individuals.

| 1 | 2 | 3 | 4 |

14 I prepare my ideas before meetings and encourage others to do likewise.

| 1 | 2 | 3 | 4 |

15 I judge alternatives against objective criteria that the decision must satisfy.

| 1 | 2 | 3 | 4 |

16 I tap every available and useful information source in and out of the organization.

| 1 | 2 | 3 | 4 |

17 I consider the actions and reactions that affect and follow from my decisions.

| 1 | 2 | 3 | 4 |

18 I weigh up probabilities when considering forecasts and planned outcomes.

| 1 | 2 | 3 | 4 |

19 I use computers where appropriate to assist in decision-making.

| 1 | 2 | 3 | 4 |

20 I seek to minimize risks, but I take necessary ones with confidence.

| 1 | 2 | 3 | 4 |

21 I use different scenarios to improve forecasts and test plans for their viability.

| 1 | 2 | 3 | 4 |

22 I make decisions on their merits and without fear for my own position.

| 1 | 2 | 3 | 4 |

23 I take care to canvass support for my decisions at all stages of the process.

| 1 | 2 | 3 | 4 |

24 I involve the whole team in drawing up plans for implementation.

| 1 | 2 | 3 | 4 |

25 I ensure that a named person is accountable for each stage of an action plan.

| 1 | 2 | 3 | 4 |

26 I communicate my decisions openly, honestly, and as quickly as possible.

| 1 | 2 | 3 | 4 |

27 I try to encourage people to come forward with any objections.

1 2 3 4

28 I put monitoring systems in place and use them to check progress.

1 2 3 4

29 I use action reviews to discover and learn the lessons of success and failure.

1 2 3 4

30 I explain my decisions clearly and ensure that they have been understood.

1 2 3 4

31 I take full responsibility for the performance of the people I decide to hire.

1 2 3 4

32 I try to ensure that all my meetings end with making clear decisions.

1 2 3 4

ANALYSIS

Now that you have completed the assessment, add up your total score and check your performance by reading the corresponding evaluation. Whatever level of success you have achieved, or have the potential to achieve, there is always room for improvement. Identify your weakest areas, then refer to the relevant sections of this book, where you will find practical advice and tips that will enable you to hone your decision-making skills.

32–63: Your decision-making is poor. Look at the areas in which you scored badly, then adopt methods you have not tried before.
64–95: Your decision-making skills are basically sound; build on them.
96–128: Your decision-making skills are strong, but do not become complacent– look to improve.

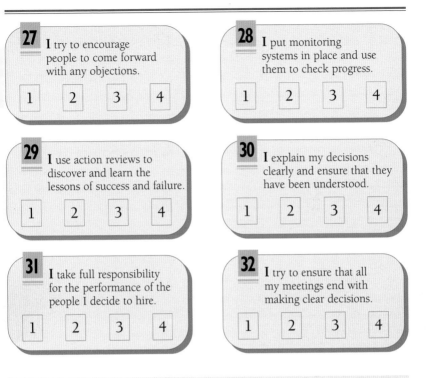

INDEX

ACKNOWLEDGMENTS

AUTHOR'S ACKNOWLEDGMENTS

This book owes its existence to the perceptive inspiration of Stephanie Jackson and Nigel Duffield at Dorling Kindersley, and I owe more than I can say to the expertise and enthusiasm of Jane Simmonds and all the editorial and design staff who worked on the project. I am also greatly indebted to the many colleagues, friends, and other management luminaries on whose wisdom and information I have drawn.

PUBLISHER'S ACKNOWLEDGMENTS

Dorling Kindersley would like to thank Emma Lawson and Jayne Jones for their valuable part in the planning and development of this series, everyone who generously lent props for the photoshoots, and the following for their help and participation:

Editorial Tracey Beresford, Deirdre Clark, Christopher Gordon, Nicola Munro;
Design Helen Benfield, Kate Poole; **DTP assistance** Rachel Symons;
Consultant Josephine Bryan; **Indexer** Hilary Bird; **Proofreader** Helen Partington;
Photography Steve Gorton; **Photographer's assistant** Sarah Ashun;
Photographic coordinator Laura Watson.

Models Philip Argent, Marian Broderick, Angela Cameron, Kuo Kang Chen, Roberto Costa, Felicity Crowe, Patrick Dobbs, Vosjava Fahkro, Ben Glickman, Richard Hill, Zahid Malik, Maggie Mant, Frankie Mayers, Sotiris Melioumis, Mutsumi Niwa, Kiran Shah, Lynne Staff, Daniel Stevens, Fiona Terry, Tessa Woodward, Wendy Yun; **Makeup** Elizabeth Burrage.

Special thanks to the following for their help throughout the series:
Ron and Chris at Clark Davis & Co. Ltd for stationery and furniture supplies; Pam Bennett and the staff at Jones Bootmakers, Covent Garden, for the loan of footwear; Alan Pfaff and the staff at Moss Bros, Covent Garden, for the loan of the men's suits; David Bailey for his help and time; Graham Preston and the staff at Staverton for their time and space.

Suppliers Austin Reed, Church & Co., Compaq, David Clulow Opticians, Elonex, Escada, Filofax, Gateway 2000, Mucci Bags.

Picture researchers Victoria Peel, Sam Ruston; **Picture library assistant** Sue Hadley.

PICTURE CREDITS

Key: *b* bottom, *c* center, *l* left, *r* right, *t* top
Pictor International, London 4–5; **Tony Stone Images:** Bruce Ayres 28*br*, Frank Herholdt 19*b*, 43*tr*, Alan Klehr 13*tl*, Ron Sherman 39*t*; **Telegraph Colour Library:** 49*tr*, Spencer Rowell 59*t*. Front cover **Pictor International, London** *cl*.

AUTHOR'S BIOGRAPHY

Robert Heller is a leading authority in the world of management consulting and was the founding editor of Britain's top management magazine, *Management Today*. He is much in demand as a conference speaker in Europe, North and South America, and the Far East. As editorial director of Haymarket Publishing Group, Robert Heller supervised the launch of several highly successful magazines such as *Campaign*, *Computing*, and *Accountancy Age*. His many acclaimed – and worldwide best-selling – books include *The Naked Manager*, *Culture Shock*, *The Age of the Common Millionaire*, *The Way to Win* (with Will Carling), *The Complete Guide to Modern Management*, and *In Search of European Excellence*.